W9-AVK-379

Major European
Union Nations

MAJOR
EUROPEAN UNION
NATIONS

Austria
Belgium
Czech Republic
Denmark
France
Germany
Greece
Ireland

Italy
The Netherlands
Poland
Portugal
Spain
Sweden
United Kingdom

ITALY

by
Ademola O. Sadek and Shaina C. Indovino

Mason Crest

Mason Crest
370 Reed Road, Broomall,
Pennsylvania 19008
www.masoncrest.com

Printed in the Hashemite Kingdom of Jordan.

First printing
9 8 7 6 5 4 3 2 1

Library of Congress Cataloging-in-Publication Data

Sadik, Ademola O.
  Italy / by Ademola O. Sadik and Shaina C. Indovino.
      p. cm. — (The European Union : political, social, and economic cooperation)
  Includes index.
  ISBN 978-1-4222-2248-5 (hardcover) — ISBN 978-1-4222-2231-7 (series hardcover) — ISBN 978-1-4222-9270-9 (ebook)

  1. Italy—Juvenile literature. 2. European Union—Italy—Juvenile literature. I. Indovino, Shaina Carmel. II. Title.
  DG467.S24 2011
  945—dc22
                                          2010051333

Produced by Harding House Publishing Services, Inc.
www.hardinghousepages.com
Interior layout by Micaela Sanna.
Cover design by Torque Advertising + Design.

CONTENTS

INTRODUCTION 8

1. MODERN ISSUES 11

2. ITALY'S HISTORY AND GOVERNMENT 19

3. THE ECONOMY 35

4. ITALY'S PEOPLE AND CULTURE 41

5. LOOKING TO THE FUTURE 49

TIME LINE 56

FIND OUT MORE 58

GLOSSARY 59

INDEX 61

PICTURE CREDITS 62

ABOUT THE AUTHORS 63

ABOUT THE CONSULTANT 64

ITALY

European Union Member
since 1952

Trieste

Milan • Verona

Torino • Venice

Parma

Genoa • Bologna

Pisa San Marino

Florence

Livorno

Vatican
City Pescara

☆ **Rome**

Foggia

Naples Bari

Salerno

Taranto

Sardinia

Cagliari

Reggio di Calabria

Messina

Palermo

Catania

Sicily

Introduction

Sixty years ago, Europe lay scarred from the battles of the Second World War. During the next several years, a plan began to take shape that would unite the countries of the European continent so that future wars would be inconceivable. On May 9, 1950, French Foreign Minister Robert Schuman issued a declaration calling on France, Germany, and other European countries to pool together their coal and steel production as "the first concrete foundation of a European federation." "Europe Day" is celebrated each year on May 9 to commemorate the beginning of the European Union (EU).

The EU consists of twenty-seven countries, spanning the continent from Ireland in the west to the border of Russia in the east. Eight of the ten most recently admitted EU member states are former communist regimes that were behind the Iron Curtain for most of the latter half of the twentieth century.

Any European country with a democratic government, a functioning market economy, respect for fundamental rights, and a government capable of implementing EU laws and policies may apply for membership. Bulgaria and Romania joined the EU in 2007. Croatia, Serbia, Turkey, Iceland, Montenegro, and Macedonia have also embarked on the road to EU membership.

While the EU began as an idea to ensure peace in Europe through interconnected economies, it has evolved into so much more today:

- Citizens can travel freely throughout most of the EU without carrying a passport and without stopping for border checks.

- EU citizens can live, work, study, and retire in another EU country if they wish.

- The euro, the single currency accepted throughout seventeen of the EU countries (with more to come), is one of the EU's most tangible achievements, facilitating commerce and making possible a single financial market that benefits both individuals and businesses.

- The EU ensures cooperation in the fight against cross-border crime and terrorism.

- The EU is spearheading world efforts to preserve the environment.

- As the world's largest trading bloc, the EU uses its influence to promote fair rules for world trade, ensuring that globalization also benefits the poorest countries.

- The EU is already the world's largest donor of humanitarian aid and development assistance, providing around 60 percent of global official development assistance to developing countries in 2011.

The EU is not a nation intended to replace existing nations. The EU is unique—its member countries have established common institutions to which they delegate some of their sovereignty so that decisions on matters of joint interest can be made democratically at the European level.

Europe is a continent with many different traditions and languages, but with shared values such as democracy, freedom, and social justice, cherished values well known to North Americans. Indeed, the EU motto is "United in Diversity."

Enjoy your reading. Take advantage of this chance to learn more about Europe and the EU!

Ambassador John Bruton,
Former EU President and Prime Minister of Ireland

CHAPTER 1

MODERN ISSUES

Back in the fifteenth century, an Italian woman named Laura Cereta laid the foundation for modern feminism. An educated woman herself, she passionately defended women's right to education, and she fought against society's oppression of women. Today, if Laura could see what's happening in her country, she'd be rolling in her grave!

WOMEN IN ITALY

Of all the nations who have joined the European Union (EU), Italy ranks among the lowest when it comes to women's rights. Only 45 percent of Italian women work outside the home, which is well below the average for the rest of the EU. In 2010, Italy ranked lower than countries like Kazakhstan and Malawi in the World Economic Forum's Global Gender Gap Report. Italian women who are employed make on average half what Italian men make, and only 7 percent of employed women occupy management positions.

Women living in Italy face unequal treatment in everyday life. Less than half of all Italian women have a job, and those that do make less than men do.

THE FORMATION OF THE EUROPEAN UNION

The EU is a confederation of European nations that continues to grow. All countries that enter the EU agree to follow common laws about foreign security policies. They also agree to cooperate on legal matters that go on within the EU. The European Council meets to discuss all international matters and make decisions about them. Each country's own concerns and interests are important, though. And apart from legal and financial issues, the EU tries to uphold values such as peace and solidarity, human dignity, freedom, and equality. All member countries remain autonomous. This means that they generally keep their own laws and regulations. The EU becomes involved only if there is an international issue or if a member country has violated the principles of the union.

The idea for a union among European nations was first mentioned after World War II. The war had devastated much of Europe, both physically and financially. In 1950, French foreign minister Robert Schuman suggested that France and West Germany combine their coal and steel industries under one authority. Both countries would have control over the industries. This would help them become more financially stable. It would also make war between the countries much more difficult. The idea was interesting to other European countries as well. In 1951, France, West Germany, Belgium, Luxembourg, the Netherlands, and Italy signed the Treaty of Paris, creating the European Coal and Steel Community. These six countries would become the core of the EU.

In 1957, these same countries signed the Treaties of Rome, creating the European Economic Community. This combined their economies into a single European economy. In 1965, the Merger Treaty brought together a number of these treaty organizations. The organizations were joined under a common banner, known as the European Community. Finally, in 1992, the Maastricht Treaty was signed. This treaty defined the European Union. It gave a framework for expanding the EU's political role, particularly in the area of foreign and security policy. It would also replace national currencies with the euro. The next year, the treaty went into effect. At that time, the member countries included the original six plus another six who had joined during the 1970s and '80s.

In the following years, the EU would take more steps to form a single market for its members. This would make joining the union even more of an advantage. Three more countries joined during the 1990s. Another twelve joined in the first decade of the twenty-first century. As of 2012, six countries were waiting to join the EU.

Back in the 1960s and '70s, Italy did have a women's rights movement, along with much of the Western world. But by the 1980s, the movement had faded away. Italian journalist Caterina Soffici has referred to her country as "the most sexist country in Europe." Italy's bad reputation got even worse in 2011, when the nation's prime minister went on trial for paying an underage prostitute for sex.

Legally, Italian women have many of the same rights as the rest of the EU. They are free to divorce, they have access to contraception, and they are technically free to pursue whatever career they want. But the reality for most women lies far from their legal rights. In Italy, women are seldom leaders, and their voices are not heard in important discussions.

Historically, Italians have had a hard time uniting to work together. The family and the local community is more important to many Italians than any bigger cause, which makes it difficult for Italian feminists to bring about any lasting change in their country. In February 2011, however, a million marchers turned out in Rome, Italy's capital city, to speak out on behalf of women's rights. Feminists hope the event indicates that Italians are finally waking up to the many serious issues women face in Italy.

Meanwhile, feminists like Lorella Zanardo are working hard to educate young Italian women, working within schools to increase their self-esteem. "I am seeing so much energy in the schools," says Lorella, and that energy gives her hope for Italy's women.

THE ROMA IN ITALY

Women aren't the only ones who have troubles in Italy; the Roma people also face **discrimination** and unequal opportunities. According to the Italian government, the nation is facing a "Gypsy emergency." Italian authorities blame Roma immigrants for Italy's rise in crime. Large Roma camps outside Milan and Rome face direct attacks from authorities. The mayor of Milan said, "Our final goal is to have zero Gypsy camps."

The EU has official policies that protect the Roma's rights. However, the EU does not interfere with city government, which is how Italy is getting away with expelling the Roma from their cities.

In April 2011, the city of Rome knocked down the homes of 150 or more Roma, who then took refuge in one of the city's ancient churches. Claiming the church's **sanctuary**, the Roma ended up in a standoff with the officials who wanted them out of the city. The city offered to send the women and children—but not the men—to shelters, but the Roma did not want their families broken up. So many people could not live forever in a church, though. Eventually, the Roma were forced to leave the building in search of food or jobs—and once they left, police kept them from going back.

Pope Benedict spoke from the **Vatican** on behalf of the Roma's rights. In his Easter message, the pope called Catholics to speak up in **solidarity** for the Roma. But Rome's mayor said, "We cannot run the risk of turning Rome into a gigantic shantytown."

Traditional Gypsy cart traveling along a modern road.

WHO ARE THE ROMA?

About a thousand years ago, groups of people migrated from northern India, spreading across Europe over the next several centuries. Though these people actually came from several different tribes (the largest of which were the Sinti and Roma), the people of Europe called them simply "Gypsies"—a shortened version of "Egyptians," since people thought they came from Egypt.

Europeans were frightened of these dark-skinned, non-Christian people who spoke a foreign language. Unlike the settled people of Europe, the Roma were wanderers, with no ties to the land. Europeans did not understand them. Stories and stereotypes grew up about the Gypsies, and these fanned the flames of prejudice and discrimination. Many of these same stories and stereotypes are still believed today.

Throughout the centuries, non-Gypsies continually tried to either assimilate the Gypsies or kill them. Attempts to assimilate the Gypsies involved stealing their children and placing them with other families; giving them cattle and feed, expecting them to become farmers; outlawing their customs, language, and clothing, and forcing them to attend school and church. In many ways the Roma of Europe were treated much as the European settlers treated the Native peoples of North America.

Many European laws allowed—or even commanded—the killing of Gypsies. A practice of "Gypsy hunting"—similar to fox hunting—was both common and legal in some parts of Europe. Even as late as 1835, a Gypsy hunt in Denmark "brought in a bag of over 260 men, women, and children." But the worst of all crimes against the Roma happened in the twentieth century, when Hitler's Third Reich sent them to concentration camps. As many as half a million Gypsies died in the Nazis' death camps.

Earlier in 2011, when four Roma children between the ages of three and eleven died in a fire in one of Rome's gypsy camps, Rome's mayor promised that the city would build new, safer homes for the Roma. Instead, the old camps are being destroyed, leaving many Roma homeless.

Issues like the ones that women and the Roma are facing are not the only serious problems in Italy. The nation's economy and its politics are also full of weaknesses and corruption. Despite that, however, the nation has a long, strong history on which to build.

The city of Venice, with its ancient canals, has many stories to add to Italy's long history.

2 ITALY'S HISTORY AND GOVERNMENT

CHAPTER

Italy has a rich history that stretches back to *prehistoric* times. During the **Neolithic** period, small agricultural-based communities replaced the hunter-gatherers of the Paleolithic and Mesolithic periods. Settlers from the east introduced the use of metal to the peninsula during the Bronze Age. With the arrival of these newcomers came distinct regional identities, which developed by 1000 BCE when the use of iron became prevalent.

Indo-European-speaking tribes began to arrive in what is now known as Italy late in the Neolithic period. These tribes, such as those speaking Latin and Venetic, settled in the peninsula but would be forced to wait their turn to exert any extensive influence over their neighbors. The **indigenous** non–Indo-European Etruscans extended a wide influence over the central portion of the peninsula and even dominated and ruled many Latin communities. Later Roman historians note that the Etruscans ruled the city of Rome for many years, and it was only after they were overthrown and

DATING SYSTEMS AND THEIR MEANING

You might be accustomed to seeing dates expressed with the abbreviations BC or AD, as in the year 1000 BC or the year AD 1900. For centuries, this dating system has been the most common in the Western world. However, since BC and AD are based on Christianity (BC stands for Before Christ and AD stands for *anno Domini*, Latin for "in the year of our Lord"), many people now prefer to use abbreviations that people from all religions can be comfortable using. The abbreviations BCE (meaning Before Common Era) and CE (meaning Common Era) mark time in the same way (for example, 1000 BC is the same year as 1000 BCE, and AD 1900 is the same year as 1900 CE), but BCE and CE do not have the same religious overtones as BC and AD.

expelled that the Latin tribes began to forge what would eventually become one of the greatest empires the world has ever known.

THE BIRTH AND GROWTH OF ROME

The mythical legend of the city of Rome's founding states that Romulus and Remus, twin sons of a Vestal Virgin raped by Mars, the god of war, founded the city, and Romulus became its first king. This account is clearly laden with mythological exaggeration, but whatever the true origin of the city, after the expulsion of their Etruscan overlords, Rome began to emerge as the premier Latin settlement, and its inhabitants began socially and militarily dominating their Latin cousins around them. The Latins lived in Latium, a plain on the western coast of the Italian Peninsula, and were loosely associated with one another in what was known as the Latin League.

As Rome grew increasingly powerful, it began to exercise a great deal of dominion over the other cities in the league. Tension rose as the rest of Latium began to

Medieval buildings are still standing throughout Italy.

fear a Roman plan to rule the entire plain and beyond. The Latin War of 340–338 BCE pitted Rome against its Latin kinsmen and resulted in a Roman victory, dissolving the Latin League and creating a senatorial government in Rome. Rome now dominated all Latin-speaking peoples and began to pose a threat to the other tribes of the peninsula.

The Etruscans, Gauls, Samnites, and other people on the peninsula engaged Rome in a series of wars between 326 BCE and 290 BCE. Known as the Samnite Wars, there were three in total, and although Rome suffered a great deal of defeats, it also displayed a great deal of resilience, eventually defeating all who wished to challenge her authority and ruling all of Italy except the Greek

cities in the south and the territory of the Gauls to the north. The subsequent Pyrrhic and Punic wars and other conflicts also found Rome victorious, leading to the defeat of her last true rival, Carthage. Rome now had the beginnings of a consolidated empire.

Julius Caesar was the greatest ruler of the Roman ***republic***. A brilliant general and politician, he extended and solidified Roman rule into the Iberian Peninsula, Britannia, and the main portions of the remainder of Europe. During these events, Rome was still a republic ruled by the Senate, many of whom believed Caesar was growing too powerful. In 44 BCE, a group of senators murdered the popular Caesar, and after a period of civil unrest, his nephew and adopted son Octavius marched on Rome and forced the Senate to name him consul. He would eventually become the first Roman emperor, after first sharing leadership with Julius Caesar's general Marc Antony and Marcus Lepidus. Under Octavius, who was renamed "Augustus," the Roman Empire expanded to rule most of the known world. This empire would last for hundreds of years until internal strife and external threats from Germanic tribes weakened the once great empire.

THE FALL OF ROME

Because of political corruption, selfish emperors, and other undermining internal factors, Rome's power began to decline. The generals of the formerly invincible army cared more for their villas and estates than their legions' well-being and success. Weakened armies meant the barbaric Germanic tribes no longer needed to live in fear of repercussions of rebellion. They began to revolt, and without competent generals abroad or a stable emperor at home (from 186 CE to 286 CE, thirty-seven different emperors ruled, and twenty-five of those were assassinated), the empire plunged into disarray. The movement of gold into the coffers of Rome slowed as Rome stopped conquering new lands, but wealthy Romans continued to spend gold on luxury items. Because of this outflow of precious metal, less gold was available for use in minting coins, and the value of minted money dropped. This caused inflation, as merchants raised the prices of their goods. All these causes, and more—such as the split of the empire into the Roman and Byzantine empires—led to the sacking of Rome in 476, during the reign of Romulus Augustus. The Roman Empire was no more.

MEDIEVAL ITALY

After the fall of Rome, the Byzantine Empire in the East continued the legacies of both Rome and Greece, but control of Italy was eventually lost to the invading Lombards. Italy once again splintered into ethnic strongholds. The Lombards, a Germanic tribe, ruled an extensive portion of the peninsula, until the **papacy** invited the Franks (another Germanic tribe) to invade Italy in order to restore land that the Church had lost. This began the rule of the Holy Roman Empire (under Charlemagne) in Europe. Around this time, Arabs from North Africa conquered Sicily, but they were eventually expelled by the Normans, who established a kingdom on the small island.

Strong **city-states** began to arise in Italy during the Middle Ages. Florence, Milan, and Venice, among others grew powerful through trade, and Italy was effectively splintered into regional rule. Strong and wealthy families in the city-states began to rule and gain influence. In 1494, two years after Italian Cristoforo Colombo (Christopher Columbus) discovered the New World, Charles VIII of France invaded Italy, ending the wars between rival city-states and beginning a long period of foreign rule. The Hapsburg Dynasty brought most of Italy under control, and when the dynasty was divided between Emperor Ferdinand I and King Phillip II of Spain, Phillip inherited Italy. In the early 1700s, Austria **annexed** Italy in the War of the Spanish Succession (1701–1714). Small parts of Italy began gaining independence from foreign rule, but the nation remained fragmented into separately ruled regions.

UNIFICATION OF ITALY

Foreign rule made the dwellers of the Italian Peninsula desire freedom. Revolutions by the Carbonari, a radical group, were **quelled** by the Austrians, as were the Revolutions of 1848, in which the king of Sardinia declared Italy free and created a constitution. In 1859, France and England saw an Austrian defeat as favorable to their political interests. Sardinia led the battle for Italian independence against Austria with the help of Giuseppe Garibaldi, who led his "Redshirts" to the southern part of the peninsula and captured it; then, showing his true patriotism, handed it over to King Emmanuel II of Sardinia. The Kingdom of Italy was formed officially in 1861.

The new nation had many internal problems. Its citizens thought of themselves not as Italians, but identified more with the region of their birth and ancestry. The country was in debt, and the pope refused to recognize the new nation, furious over the seizure of papal lands. The northern portion of the country developed to a greater extent than the southern portion. Crime and social activism increased as the poorer south seemed stuck in its misery. The people were for the most part poor and illiterate, and the nation had nothing in terms of international prestige or recognition. In an attempt to gain status as a colonial power, Italy foolishly attacked the stronger African nation of Ethiopia and was embarrassed on an international level as they were defeated soundly in the 1890s. It apparently failed to learn its lesson as Italy went on to declare war on Turkey over the North African nation of Libya in 1911. During World War I, Italy joined the Allies only to suffer staggering losses of men and machines during the course of the war. The postwar failure of the Allies to provide lands that Italy had been promised on joining the Allied war effort led to a generally disgruntled Italian

Italy's past and present are mixed together in the village of Portofino.

population, laying down the foundations for Benito Mussolini and fascism to take control of the nation.

THE RISE OF FASCISM

Benito Mussolini began the fascist movement in Italy. His "Blackshirts," a squad of thugs who ter-rorized those whose views differed from Mussolini, helped him gain strength in the troubled nation. King Victor Emmanuel III named Mussolini prime minister in 1922, and within several years, the nation had been transformed into a military state by the new regime. In 1935, Mussolini sent troops back to Ethiopia to compensate for the embarrassing military fiasco of the 1890s, and

Italy's modern politics are visible on a Genoa street wall.

Liguria migliore.

Maria Grazia Barbieri

Fra noi il

UMBERTO CALCAGNO
VICE SEGRETARIO REGIONALE
CONSIGLIERE NAZIONALE UDC

the following year Italian troops were sent to Spain to aid Francisco Franco in the Spanish Civil War. German dictator Adolf Hitler formed the Rome-Berlin Pact in 1936, and both dictators continued to **satiate** their aggressive land-seizing propensities as Hitler annexed Alsace-Lorraine and the Sudetenland, while Mussolini added Albania to Italy's territory. The English prime minister Neville Chamberlain and his French allies continued to **appease** the two obvious threats, and the result of this was the outbreak of World War II, when Hitler attacked Poland, with Mussolini joining the war on the German side several months later.

WORLD WAR II

During World War II, Italy's meager conquests were generally overshadowed by the stronger successes of the German *blitzkrieg*, or lightning war. The overall incompetence of Italy's army was an embarrassing contrast to Rome's past military prowess. The Allies invaded Italy in 1943, and Mussolini was expelled to a puppet government in the northern part of the nation after King Victor Emmanuel III forced him to resign. Mussolini was captured and executed by communist partisans during the final stages of the Allied expulsion of the German army from Italy.

POSTWAR ITALY

The monarchy was abolished in 1946 and a new republican constitution was drafted. The United States gave a great deal of aid to Italy as a part of the **Marshall Plan**, and because of this, the Italian economy grew considerably. Industrial expansion and economic growth resulted in a higher standard of living for the average Italian citizen. However, the 1970s saw a return to labor unrest and political agitation. Extremist groups seemed to be on the rise until the mid- to late 1980s under the premiership of Bettino Craxi, when the economy made a recovery.

THE ITALIAN GOVERNMENT

Today, the Italian form of government is a republic. Universal **suffrage** has been granted to all citizens over the age of eighteen, but for senatorial elections, the minimum age requirement is twenty-five years of age. The executive branch of the government consists of the president, the Council of Ministers, and the prime minister, who is also the president of the Council of Ministers. The Italian parliament and fifty-eight regional representatives form an electoral college that elects the president for a seven-year term. The president in turn nominates a prime minister, who must be approved by parliament. He also nominates a Council of Ministers to preside over and be approved by the president.

The Leaning Tower of Pisa

The *parlamento*, or parliament, is comprised of the *Senato della Repubblica*, or Senate, and the *Camera dei Deputati*, or Chamber of Deputies, in a **bicameral** configuration. There are a number of senators for life, a classification all former presidents are placed in. The senators serve five-year terms, as do legislators in the Chamber of Deputies.

The judicial branch of the government is composed of the *Corte Costituzionale*, or Constitutional Court. This court has five judges appointed by the president, five elected by the parliament, and five elected from Supreme Courts.

President Giorgio Napolitano started serving in 2006, and Prime Minister Mario Monti has headed Italy since November 2011. There are myriad political parties in the government with many parties forming coalitions with other parties, creating party conglomerates such as the Daisy Alliance, which was formed by the Italian Popular Party, the Italian Renewal Party, the Union of Democrats for Europe, and the Democrats.

ITALY AND THE EUROPEAN UNION

Italy is a founding member of the EU, and has held the presidency of the EU eleven times. As an original member, Italy holds an important position in the EU, and it has been a strong supporter of the EU. However, it does not always agree with other European nations as to how the EU's government should function.

One of the big issues in the EU is similar to one that the United States faces as well: who should have more power, the central government (the EU in Europe, or Washington, D.C., in the United States) or the individual members (the nations of Europe or the states of the United States)?

THE TOWER OF PISA

One of Italy's most recognizable sights is the Tower of Pisa. The bell tower of the city's cathedral, it sits in Pisa's *Campo dei Miracoli*, Field of Miracles.

Work began on the tower in 1173 and continued for almost two hundred years, with a couple of long interruptions. For many years, it was believed that the leaning was a "design element," but it is now known that the tower was meant to stand erect. The leaning began during the building, and many construction mechanisms were tried to prevent the tilt. Nothing worked. Efforts are still under way to stop the inclination from progressing. Today's efforts are focused on the subsoil beneath and around the tower.

Even if the tower was straight, it would still be one of the most impressive sites in the country. But, there wouldn't be the traditional photographs of tourists holding up the tower to keep it from falling.

Fast Facts About the Tower of Pisa

The Tower of Pisa is 180.4 feet (55 meters) tall, weighs approximately 14,500 tons, and has 294 steps.

Italy's national flag flying next to the flag of the European Union.

While the European Union does act as a unifier between its members, conflict exists as to who has the absolute power when making final legislation.

When all the EU members' governments have to agree before any member can take action, that's known as intergovernmentalism; everyone works together to form the central government's laws and policies. In the EU, the opposite approach is called supranationalism, which is where the member countries make their own decisions regarding many laws and policies, but also where the EU as a whole can make decisions for all its members, whether they agree or not. The EU uses both these methods, but some EU nations generally support one approach over the other. Italy

The Palazzo Montecitorio is a palace in Rome, which is currently the seat of the Italian Chamber of Deputies.

has supported a supranational approach, along with several other European nations, notably France. Other European nations nations support an approach that allows them more individual choice.

The conflict between these two approaches often becomes more obvious when smaller issues arise. In the United States, it came to a head in the 1800s over the issue of slavery, causing the Civil War, but it continues to be an important question whenever states don't agree on a particular issue, such as same-sex marriage or abortion rights. The smaller issues in Europe are different (they often have to do with the rights of ethnic minorities, with the environment, and with money), but the big issue is very much the same. Will the EU be able to unite its power the way the United States did—or will it continue to act as many separate nations? That question still hasn't been settled.

MODERN POLITICS IN ITALY

From 1994 to 2011, Italy's three-time prime minister, Silvio Berlusconi, an eccentric billionaire, controlled its politics. Although Berlusconi's final term was supposed to end in 2012, Italians seemed to have grown tired of him by the end of 2010, and he resigned in 2011. The former prime minister has been involved in many scandals, including criminal charges for paying for sex with an underage woman and then abusing his office's power to help release her after she was arrested for theft. Critics of Berlusconi also point to his mismanagement as part of the cause for Italy's economic crisis.

Unfortunately, Italy has always had problems acting as a unified whole, which makes it difficult for real change to come to this beautiful and historic nation. Most Italians identify far more with their family, town, or local region than they do with their nation as a whole—and few Italians identify with the EU at all. This has made Italy's politics **fragmented** and **ineffective**; since World War II, the country has had more than sixty different governments, each one rising and falling, with little **continuity** between them. With so many starts and stops, it's hard for the nation to make progress!

Because of this, Italy faces many dilemmas. Its economy is one of its biggest problems—and yet despite that, Italians enjoy one of the world's highest standards of living. Italy's fashion, luxury cars and motorcycles, furniture, tourism, design, and food still help set the entire world's standards.

The Italian Riviera along the Mediterranean Coast attracts many tourists.

3 THE ECONOMY

Since the unification of Italy in 1861, the northern regions of Italy have always enjoyed greater prosperity and industrial viability than the southern regions. The southern, more agricultural region lacks the industry and private companies that the north has always possessed. Italy's natural resources include coal, zinc, and marble, and the surrounding presence of water has allowed the fishing industry to grow.

Quick Facts: The Economy of Italy

Gross Domestic Product (GDP): US$1.822 trillion (2011 est.)
GDP per capita: US$30,100 (2011 est.)
Industries: tourism, machinery, iron and steel, chemicals, food processing, textiles, motor vehicles, clothing, footwear, ceramics
Agriculture: fruits, vegetables, grapes, potatoes, sugar beets, soybeans, grain, olives, beef, dairy products, fish
Export commodities: engineering products, textiles and clothing, production machinery, motor vehicles, transport equipment, chemicals; food, beverages and tobacco; minerals, and nonferrous metals
Export partners: Germany 13%, France 11.6%, US 6%, Spain 5.9%, UK 5.2%, Switzerland 4.7% (2011 est.)
Import commodities: engineering products, chemicals, transport equipment, energy products, minerals and nonferrous metals, textiles and clothing; food, beverages, and tobacco
Import partners: Germany 16.1%, France 8.8%, China 7.8%, Netherlands 5.4%, Spain 4.6% (2011 est.)
Currency: euro (EUR)
Currency exchange rate: US$1 = €.7107 (2011)

Note: All figures are from 2011 unless otherwise noted.
Source: www.cia.gov, 2012.

In 2011, Italy's **gross domestic product (GDP)** was US$1.822 trillion. The 2011 per capita GDP, the country's total GDP divided into the total population was US$30,100. The main sources of Italy's GDP are 72.9 percent from the **service sector**, 25.2 percent from industry, and 1.9 percent from agriculture.

The employment of Italy's labor force of 25.05 million reflects the importance of the service sector and industrial sector to Italy's economy. Approximately 68 percent of the workforce is employed in the service sector, and about 28 percent work in industry. Only about 4 percent of the workforce is employed in agriculture-related occupations.

Italy's major industries include tourism, chemical production, textiles and design of fine apparel, and motor vehicle production. The predominant agricultural products generated in Italy are beef, dairy products, fruits and vegetables, and fish.

Some of Italy's main trading partners are Germany, France, Spain, and the United States. Among Italy's lucrative exports are luxury cars; Italy is a world leader in their production. Car companies such as Ferrari, Alfa Romeo, Maserati, Fiat, and Lancia are exported to almost every country in the world. These expensive cars have given Italy a reputation for fine things over

Fishing plays a part in Italy's economy.

the years; many of these car companies date back to the early 1900s.

Most of Italy's energy needs must be met by imports; Italy produces only 146,500 barrels per day (bbl/day) of oil, while consuming 1.573 million bbl/day. The nation also produces 8.119 billion cubic meters of natural gas and consumes 78.12 billion cubic meters of natural gas. Much of the oil and gas required for Italy is imported. Italy has 769 miles (1,241 kilometers) of crude oil pipeline and 11,373 miles (18,343 kilometers) of natural gas pipeline.

THE COST OF RECESSION

Many Italians feel desperate and frustrated about their country's economy. In 2012, two workers felt so upset, in fact, that they set themselves on fire with gasoline, in two separate incidents. Both men said they simply could not afford to live.

Meanwhile, Prime Minister Mario Monti's government was cracking down on tax dodging and increasing austerity measures, including tax raises, spending cuts, and pension changes. These changes make it easier for employers to let go of workers. Experts say that all these changes weigh extra hard on ordinary workers.

Vincenzo Scudiere from one of Italy's trade unions said the workers' self-immolation was a "symptom of the utter exasperation felt by the weakest employees," and warned the government not to underestimate how unhappy Italian workers truly are.

Italy is known for its impressive rail system that provides transportation througout the country and its neighbors.

Since the construction of its first railroad in 1839, Italy has developed its rail system into one of the most impressive in Europe. Most rail stations in Italy are famous for their beautiful architecture. Italy has international rail links to France, Austria, Switzerland, and Slovenia and, in 2005, began plans for possibly building an underwater subway system from Sicily to Tunisia.

With 302,374 miles (487,700 kilometers) of roadways, over-the-road transport of goods is easily accomplished. Italy has many harbors and ports along coastline, and 132 airports, making ship and air transport viable options as well.

ITALY'S ECONOMY AND THE GLOBAL RECESSION

In 2008, the United States economy entered a slowdown period. Many companies made less money or went out of business all together. As a result, there were fewer jobs, and unemployment soared. Because many people were out of work, they had less money to spend, which meant that businesses did even worse, creating a vicious circle that led to what **economists** call a recession. And because the economies of the world are so linked together, with nations trading with each other and many businesses operating in countries all around the world, the recession soon spread from the United States around the globe. As a result, the EU's economy also entered a recession. Italy was one of the European nations that was in the biggest trouble.

Other EU countries—like Greece, Portugal, and Ireland—might have had worse problems, but Italy's economy was more important to both the EU and the entire world, so in a way, its economic problems were more frightening. The Italian economy is the seventh largest in the world, which means that when Italy has problems, those problems affect many other nations as well. During the EU's recession, UniCredit, a European banking group, said that Italy was "the swing factor" that would determine how well the EU emerged from the recession. Italy, said UniCredit, was "the largest of the **vulnerable** countries, and most vulnerable of the large" nations in the EU. By 2010 and beyond, most of the EU was coming out of the recession, but economists are still keeping a worried eye on Italy.

Many experts point to Italy's culture as being partly responsible for its economic problems. Just as Italy has had trouble uniting socially and politically, it also has trouble working together toward common economic goals. Italians are loyal to their individual communities, and even more loyal to their own families. They protect what they see as their family's, even at the cost of hurting their nation as a whole. Many businesses are controlled by family-run **guilds** that keep outsiders out of the jobs. Italian businesspeople tend to care very little about growth; they hate risk; and they want to keep things exactly the way they've always been. As a result, people who do not belong to a rich, powerful family often have few opportunities, and many of the best and brightest young people are leaving Italy altogether.

All this makes for an outdated and shaky economy that may not be able to survive the challenges of the twenty-first century. And yet Italy has a rich culture that could help make it strong.

The sea has an important role in Italy's culture.

4 ITALY'S PEOPLE AND CULTURE

Many different ethnicities and cultures are represented among the 58 million inhabitants of Italy. This is in part due to the almost perpetual foreign rule that the nation has been under for much of its history. Recent immigration has added to the country's rich diversity. The majority of people are Italian, but there are clusters of German-Italians, Greek-Italians, French-Italians, and Slovene-Italians.

QUICK FACTS: THE PEOPLE OF ITALY

Population: 61,261,254 (July 2012 est.)

Ethnic groups: Italian (includes small clusters of German-, French-, and Slovene-Italians in the north and Albanian-Italians and Greek-Italians in the south)

Age structure:
 0–14 years: 13.8%
 15–64 years: 65.9%
 65 years and over: 20.3%

Population growth rate: 0.38% (2012 est.)

Birth rate: 9.06 births/1,000 population (2012 est.)

Death rate: 9.93 deaths/1,000 population (July 2012 est.)

Migration rate: 4.67 migrant(s)/1,000 population (2012 est.)

Infant mortality rate: 3.36 deaths/1,000 live births

Life expectancy at birth:
 Total population: 81.86 years
 Male: 79.24 years
 Female: 84.63 years (2012 est.)

Total fertility rate: 1.4 children born/woman (2012 est.)

Religions: Roman Catholic 90% (approximately; about one-third practicing), other 10% (includes mature Protestant and Jewish communities and a growing Muslim immigrant community)

Languages: Italian, German, French, Slovene

Literacy rate: 98.4% (2003 estimate)

Note: All figures are from 2011 unless otherwise noted.
Source: www.cia.gov, 2012.

descendants of the Greeks who in ancient times migrated to and colonized the portions of Italy that became known as Magna Grecia; they speak Griko, a language descending from Greek.) The island of Sicily's inhabitants are ethnically a mix of Italians, Greeks, Phoenicians, and Arabs; some also have Norman, Spanish, and Albanian ancestry. Sicilian is a distinct ***Romance language*** spoken by most of its inhabitants, although it is spoken less and less as a first language, since the Italian spoken in public schools takes precedence among the youth.

A large influx of recent, mostly illegal immigrants from the continent of Africa is increasing the ethnic diversity of Italy. Although mainly from North African nations, there is an increasing number of Italians of Sub-Saharan origin living primarily in large cities such as Rome. The North African immigration is increasing Italy's Muslim population.

The persecution of Kurds in Turkey in recent years has caused an increase in Kurdish migration to Italy. Italy has been criticized by

Most ethnic groups are bilingual, speaking Italian along with their native languages. (The Greek-Italians in the southern regions and Sicily are

other EU member states such as Germany on its seemingly open-door policy toward unauthorized Kurdish immigration. These EU member states claim that illegal Kurdish immigration to Italy, when coupled with the open borders among all EU nations, results in a wave of illegal Kurdish immigration to other EU nations, immigration the other nations may not be able to accommodate.

Most of Italy's population is Roman Catholic. However, the Protestant, Jewish, and Muslim communities are small but growing.

THE ARTS

Italy has a rich history of art, architecture, and literature. In the fourteenth century, the Renaissance

Italians are politically active.

An Italian woman pedals home with her shopping.

began in Italy. Beginning in the city of Florence in northern Italy, the Renaissance spread to the remainder of Italy and then to the rest of Europe, effectively ending the Dark Ages. The Renaissance, which means "rebirth" in French, was a period in which new ways of thinking and new artistic and literary methods of expressing those new thoughts were developed. Italy holds an illustrious place among those countries that produced well-known Renaissance thinkers. Works from influential thinkers such as Machiavelli, author of *The Art of War* and *The Prince*, and art from the likes of Michelangelo, who created the famous nude statue of the Hebrew King David and the ceiling **frescoes** of Rome's Sistine Chapel, are renowned worldwide. The futuristic designs of Leonardo da Vinci, whose notebooks even contain plans for a rudimentary helicopter, and his world-famous artworks including *Mona Lisa* and *The Last Supper*, were also among the products of the Italian Renaissance.

Italy is widely known as the birthplace of opera. Traditionally, most opera is performed in Italian. Opera was exported to other nations in Europe, and the result is many non-Italian composers have written operas. However, Italians such as Giuseppe Verdi and Giacomo Puccini remain favorites of opera lovers worldwide.

Another Italian contribution to music is the invention of the pianoforte, or piano, some time in the late 1600s by Bartolomeo Cristoforo of Florence. The piano would soon develop into the primary instrument of composers in the latter part of the Baroque period, lasting through the Classical period. Some of the most beautiful pieces in the European musical repertoire are written for piano.

The Italian influence extends to music notation. All performance instructions are written in Italian. For example, the notation instructing the individual

Did You Know?

You can't get Parmesan cheese or Chianti wine just anywhere, and many countries are urging the passage of international laws to prevent attaching names such as Parmesan or Chianti to cheese and wine produced outside a particular region. To be truly Parmesan cheese, it must be produced in the Parma region of Italy. Chianti wine is produced only from grapes grown in the Chianti region of Tuscany.

playing the music to play loudly is *forte*, the Italian word for loud.

Today's Italian youth listen to a variety of musical genres. Italian rap and hip-hop are enjoying a considerable growth in popularity as Italian artists decide to venture into these wildly popular American genres for themselves. Rock and roll is another import of American origin, with Italian stars such as Zucchero enjoying immense popularity not only in Italy but in the rest of Europe also. Traditional folk artists also are popular among all ages in Italy, and Patchanka, an Italian mix of punk, reggae, and rock, often with politically charged lyrics, is another frequently heard musical genre.

Grand Canal at night.

RECREATION AND LEISURE

Italians love sports, both as spectators and participants. Association football, known as "football" in much of the world and as "soccer" in the United States, is the most popular sport in Italy. In Italy, football is a religion, each stadium is a Mount Olympus, and every player is a god. Italy has won the World Cup, the world championship, four times.

Italy has developed a cultural reputation as a world leader in fine clothing and luxury cars. Italian designers such as Gucci, Fendi, Prada, Salvatore Ferragamo, and Dolce and Gabanna lead the world in producing the **opulent** clothing and accessories worn by the rich and famous. Italian manufacturers such as Maserati and Ferrari dominate the luxury car field, each producing luxury cars with features once thought possible only in science fiction.

HOLIDAYS

Because most of the Italian population is Roman Catholic, many of the holidays and festivals that are a major part of Italian culture are based in Catholicism. Holidays and festivals, such as Christmas, Epiphany, and St. Stephen's Day, are all celebrated in accordance to Roman Catholic tradition.

People around the world love pasta and tomato sauce . . . Gucci designer bags . . . and the art of da Vinci and Michelangelo. Italy's food, art, and style all enrich the entire world.

CUISINE

When it comes to food, Italy's reputation for **gastronomic** delights is world famous. Italian contributions to the world of cuisine include pizza and pastas such as spaghetti and linguine. Italian breads and soups are known for their heartiness. Wine and cheese are other popular Italian exports. The country is also home to a wide selection of sausages. Two of the most famous are bologna, a seasoned sausage of mixed meats originating in the Italian city that shares its name, and salami, another seasoned sausage.

5 LOOKING TO THE FUTURE

Italy's future is uncertain. The solution to almost all its problems—women's rights, politics, the economy—all rely on whether Italians can begin to work together toward common goals.

Ultimately, however, one of the biggest issues facing the entire world has to do with global climate change. The economy of every nation in the world depends on the health of our planet in order to thrive. If the nations of the world fail to make caring for the Earth a priority, we will all suffer. Since Italians have always cared more about their own families and villages than they do the world at large, environmentalists are watching Italy to see how it will respond to the crisis of worldwide climate change. Will Italians take action to protect the environment and invest in **sustainable** forms of energy? Or will they stick their heads in the sand and insist on keeping things just as they have always been?

Many Italian communities are in fact making big changes to the way they get their energy. More than eight hundred cities and villages in Italy have built renewable-energy plants that make more energy than they use. This means that the communities actually earn money every year by selling their surplus energy. They then invest the funds back in their own communities. So in this case, Italians' tendency to focus on the smaller community versus the nation is actually helping the environment.

Unfortunately, this also means that Italy as whole lacks a consistent energy policy. Italy has many renewable energy sources available to it, including **geothermal**, solar, wind, and **hydroelectric**, but

EUROPEAN UNION—ITALY

While Italy does have easily available wind energy, the country only gets 7 percent of all its energy from renewable sources.

Italy is facing the national debate on whether or not to begin building nuclear power plants as a source of renewable energy for the country.

when experts look at the nation as a whole (instead of at individual communities), they see that only 7 percent of Italy's entire energy comes from renewable sources.

Italy's government is currently considering building nuclear power plants. The 2011 Fukushima nuclear disaster in Japan has worried Italians, though, so the government has decided to wait a year or two before pursuing its nuclear plans. Prime Minister Berlusconi has said, however, that he is "convinced that nuclear is an inescapable destiny." Concerned Italians, especially young people, are asking the government to provide them with more information before going forward.

The government will have to allow Italians a chance to vote on whether they want nuclear power plants built in their county. In a ***referendum*** held in 1987, 80 percent of Italians voted against nuclear power. This vote came shortly after the Chernobyl disaster in Russian, where a failed nuclear reactor released radiation across Europe, causing thousands if not millions of cases of cancer. The more recent disaster in Japan has some Italians convinced that nuclear plants can never be absolutely safe.

Big businesses in Italy would, however, benefit from the availability of cheap energy, and the current government hopes to use this to bolster Italy's faltering economy. Meanwhile, other experts insist that renewable energy plants would achieve the same goal, while at the same time stimulating Italy's scientific research and develop-

Italy's road toward the future looks optimistic.

Nuclear Energy Pros and Cons

People who are in favor of building nuclear plants point to the fact that the world's oil, coal, and gas supplies are running out. What's more, only a few countries have these resources, which means that countries that don't have their own oil or gas must depend on importing them from the countries that do. Nuclear plants provide jobs, promote research and development, and stimulate the economy.

People who are against building nuclear plants say that these plants are expensive to build; they require uranium, a very rare and expensive chemical element, which means that most countries will still need to depend on imports from other countries in order to get the necessary uranium; and most important, nuclear plants produce radioactive waste. When something goes wrong—as it did at Chernobyl and Fukushima—these plants release dangerous radiation into the environment. Even if nothing ever goes wrong, the radioactive waste must be collected and then permanently contained in a safe way that does not endanger the environment, a problem that has not yet been totally solved.

ment community, which is currently lagging behind the rest of the world.

In 2011, some 300,000 Italians demonstrated in Rome against the government's plans to build new nuclear plants in their land. Some experts wonder if this might be Italians' opportunity to join together in a new way, to speak out with a unified voice to both their government and the entire world on one of the most important issues that faces the future of the entire world: sustainable energy.

If Italians start working together, who knows what they might accomplish?

TIME LINE

753 BCE	According to legend, twins Romulus and Remus found Rome.
509 BCE	The Roman Republic begins.
340–338 BCE	Rome and its Latin kinsmen battle for the right to dominate Latium.
334–264 BCE	Rome begins to spread its colonial influence to the rest of the Italian Peninsula; Rome begins to mint coins.
289–275 BCE	Rome goes to war with Pyrrhus.
241 BCE	Sicily is made a Roman province.
238 BCE	Sardinia and Corsica are made Roman provinces.
49–44 BCE	Julius Caesar becomes head of Roman Republic; he is assassinated in 44 BCE.
27 BCE	Augustus Caesar becomes emperor of Rome.
43 CE	Romans occupy Britannia (Britain).
79	Mount Vesuvius erupts, burying the ancient city of Pompeii in ash.
313	Roman emperor Constantine declares Christianity the official religion of the empire and ends persecution of Christians.
476	Rome falls.
773–774	Charlemagne conquers Italy.
827	Arabs invade Sicily, and capture the island in 902.
1061–1091	Normans conquer Italy.
1252	First gold coins minted in Europe are made in Florence.
1348–1349	The Black Plague ravages Italy.

1378	The Great Schism begins.
1414–1418	The Council of Constance ends the Great Schism.
1452	Leonardo da Vinci is born in Anchiano, Italy.
1508–1512	Michelangelo paints the ceiling of the Sistine Chapel.
1633	Astronomer and scientist Galileo is condemned in Rome.
1861	The Kingdom of Italy is founded with King Emmanuel II of Sardinia as king.
1911–1912	Italy conquers Libya.
1915	Italy enters World War I on the side of the Allies.
1922	Mussolini is named prime minister of Italy; fascist rule begins.
1940	Italy enters World War II on the side of the Axis.
1944	The Allies take Rome.
1945	World War II ends.
1946	The monarchy is abolished, and the Republic of Italy is formed.
1949	Italy joins NATO.
1992	The European Union begins, with Italy as one of its founding members.
1994	Silvio Berlusconi takes control of Italian politics.
2008	The world enters a recession.
2011	An earthquake damages the Fukushima nuclear plant in Japan, releasing dangerous radiation into the environment, giving Italians second thoughts about building nuclear plants in their own country. Berlusconi resigns as prime minister.

FIND OUT MORE

IN BOOKS

Bisignano, Alphonse. *Cooking the Italian Way*. Minneapolis, Minn.: Lerner Publishing Group, 2001.
Koelihoffer, Tara. *The History of Nations: Italy*. Farmington Hills, Mich.: Thomson Gale, 2003.
Marston, Elsa. *The Byzantine Empire*. New York: Benchmark Books, 2002.
Pavlovic, Zoran. *Italy*. Northborough, Mass.: Chelsea House, 2003.

ON THE INTERNET

Travel Information
www.italiantourism.com
www.italy-travel-information.com

History and Geography
www.arcaini.com/ITALY/ItalyHistory/ItalyHistory.html
workmall.com/wfb2001/italy/italy_history_index.html

Culture and Festivals
www.globalvolunteers.org/1main/italy/italyculture.htm
www.justitaly.org/italy/italy-festivals.asp

Economic and Political Information
www.cia.gov/library/publications/the-world-factbook/geos/it.html

EU Information
europa.eu.int

Publisher's note:
The websites listed on this page were active at the time of publication. The publisher is not responsible for websites that have changed their addresses or discontinued operation since the date of publication. The publisher will review and update the website list upon each reprint.

58

GLOSSARY

annexed: Took over a territory and incorporate it into another political entity.

appease: To pacify someone, especially by giving in to demands.

bicameral: Having two separate lawmaking assemblies.

city-states: Independent states consisting of a sovereign city and its surrounding territory.

continuity: The ability to proceed without being interrupted.

discrimination: Treating people unequally and unfairly because of their race, gender, or religion.

economists: Experts who study the economy (everything to do with a country's finances, including businesses, jobs, and wealth).

fragmented: Broken into separate pieces.

frescoes: Paintings done on ceilings or walls in watercolor on fresh, damp plaster.

gastronomic: Relating to the art and appreciation of preparing and eating good food.

geothermal: Having to do with heat from the Earth.

gross domestic product (GDP): The total value of all goods and services produced in a country in a year, minus net income from investments in other countries.

guilds: Associations of people of the same trade or pursuits, formed to protect mutual interests and maintain standards.

hydroelectric: Having to do with electricity made from waterpower.

indigenous: Native to an area.

ineffective: Unable to accomplish much.

Marshall Plan: A program of loans and other economic assistance provided by the U.S. government between 1947 and 1952 to help western European nations rebuild after World War II.

Neolithic: The latest period of the Stone Age, approximately 8000 BCE to 5000 BCE.

opulent: Characterized by an obvious, lavish display of wealth.

papacy: The government of the Roman Catholic Church, headed by the pope.

prehistoric: Before the time when history was recorded in written form.

quelled: Brought something to an end, often by force.

referendum: A general vote by the people on a single political question that has been referred to them for a direct decision.

republic: A form of government in which people elect representatives to vote on their behalf.

Romance language: A language that has descended from Latin.

sanctuary: A place of safety and protection.

satiate: To satisfy a hunger completely.

service sector: Businesses that sell a service rather than a product.

solidarity: A united stand.

suffrage: The right to vote.

sustainable: Able to maintained and renewed indefinitely.

Vatican: A separate city within Rome that is the administrative center of the Roman Catholic Church and the residence of the pope.

vulnerable: Exposed to the risk of danger or harm.

INDEX

agriculture 36
Augustus, Romulus 23

Bronze Age 19
Byzantine Empire 23

Caesar, Augustus (Octavius) 23
Caesar, Julius 23
city-states 24
Cristoforo, Bartolomeo 24, 45
cuisine 46

dating systems 20

economy 13, 17, 27, 33, 35–39, 49–53, 55
Emmanuel II of Sardinia, King 24–27
energy 14, 36, 37, 50–55
Etruscans 20, 22
European Union (EU) 12–17, 29–33, 39, 43

fascism 26
fashion 33
Ferdinand I 24

Garibaldi, Giuseppe ("Redshirts") 24
government, contemporary form of 27–33
Gypsies 14–17

Hitler, Adolf 17, 27

industry 35, 36

Kingdom of Italy 24
Kurds (Turkey) 42

Latin League 20, 22
Latin War, the 22
Leonardo (da Vinci) 45, 47
Lombards 23

Machiavelli 45

Marshall Plan 27
medieval Italy 23–24
Michelangelo 45, 47
Milan 14, 24
music 35
Mussolini, Benito ("Blackshirts") 26, 27

Neolithic period 19, 20
nuclear energy 50–55

opera 45

Phillip II, King 24
postwar Italy 27
Puccini, Giacomo 45
Punic War 23
Pyrrhic War 23

Renaissance 43, 45
renewable energy 50–55
Roma 14–17
Roman Catholic Church 14, 42, 43, 47
Roman Empire 23, 24
Rome 13, 14, 17, 20–23, 27, 42, 55,

Samnite Wars 23
service sector 36
sports 47

Tower of Pisa 28–29

unification 24, 35

Verdi, Giuseppe 45
Victor Emmanuel III, King 26, 27

War of the Spanish Succession 24
women in Italy 12, 14
World War I 24
World War II 13, 27, 33

PICTURE CREDITS

ABOUT THE AUTHORS

Nigerian-born Ademola Sadik first visited Italy as a young child en route to Australia, where he and his family resided for several years. Future relocations would lead him to Las Vegas and finally to Upstate New York. With several members of his family living in Italy, Ademola contacts them via phone and Internet on a semiregular basis.

Shaina Carmel Indovino is a writer and illustrator living in Nesconset, New York. She graduated from Binghamton University, where she received degrees in sociology and English. Shaina has enjoyed the opportunity to apply both of her fields of study to her writing, and she hopes readers will benefit from taking a look at the countries of the world through more than one perspective.

ABOUT THE CONSULTANT

Ambassador John Bruton served as Irish Prime Minister from 1994 until 1997. As prime minister, he helped turn Ireland's economy into one of the fastest-growing in the world. He was also involved in the Northern Ireland Peace Process, which led to the 1998 Good Friday Agreement. During his tenure as Ireland's prime minister, he also presided over the European Union presidency in 1996 and helped finalize the Stability and Growth Pact, which governs management of the euro. Before being named the European Commission Head of Delegation in the United States, he was a member of the convention that drafted the European Constitution, signed October 29, 2004.

The European Commission Delegation to the United States represents the interests of the European Union as a whole, much as ambassadors represent their countries' interests to the U.S. government. Matters coming under European Commission authority are negotiated between the commission and the U.S. administration.